JENNY OLDFIELD

Rings On Her Fingers
LD693B
ISBN 1 85503 161 2

First published 1992

LDA, Duke Street, Wisbech, Cambs, PE13 2AE

1

Money Down the Drain

Jaz knew his mum was fooling around with Dennis on the front-room settee. The door was shut. It was 11 o'clock in the morning!

He went up to his room.

'That you, James?' Her voice sounded far off. He didn't bother to answer. She didn't bother to come out and look.

Dennis's car was parked by the kerb – a big, fat estate with fifty grand on the clock. He drove around the country, did Dennis. Jaz went up and sat on his bed and bit his nails. Then he changed out of his stupid school shirt and tie. He turned some music on loud. Music drowned your worst thoughts if you played it loud enough.

But skiving was boring if you did it by yourself. Sure, you got the buzz of actually nicking out of school. Jaz had 'got lost' on D floor between

Maths and English. He hung around for five minutes in the boys' toilets, then nipped out by the caretaker's room and across the games field. There was just enough risk of getting caught to make it exciting. Jaz made it without any trouble, though.

Then after that there was just sitting on your bed, blotting out the sound of the settee springs going like crazy.

Jaz saw himself in the mirror, pale and grey in the face. He did a few press-ups. The last games lesson he went to was before Christmas. Twenty press-ups left him breathless. Sod that. It was still only 12 o'clock and the front-room door was still tight shut.

They deserve anything they get, Jaz thought as he crept back down the stairs. Dennis's grey leather jacket was hung on a peg in the passage, keys in the right-hand pocket, wallet in the left. Jaz slipped his hand into the soft lining, grasped the flat, square shape and pulled it out. He flipped the wallet open, thumbed through credit cards and phone cards, then unzipped the section where Dennis kept his cash. The smell of leather filled his nostrils. He pulled out three notes – two twenties and a ten – flipped the wallet shut. He shoved it back into the pocket. His heart was going like the beats of a drum in a heavy rock band. The door slammed as he made his escape.

'James?' Heather heard the door go. She came charging into the hallway, yelling upstairs. No reply. 'If that kid's skiving again, I'll kill him!' she told Dennis.

Dennis was smoothing down his hairstyle in the front-room. 'Hm,' he said, looking at his watch.

Jaz was out in the town when he should have been drawing a logo for the school minibus in CDT. That cheered him up. That and the fifty quid in his jeans pocket. He started to grin. He was a kid in an old leather jacket, nipping down an alley at the back of Woolworths. He was kid of 14 trying to look 18 when he called in at the newspaper shop for fags. 'Hello, James, what happened to school today?' the nosey old bag from next door asked.

'Teachers' training day,' he lied. When he grinned he looked dead charming – and he knew it. He switched on his grin for Mrs Thompson, but he didn't stop. He headed downhill towards the canal.

There was an old factory down there that had been boarded up. It had made big metal sections for central heating, and rusting heaps of the stuff still lay about the yard. It was overgrown with weeds, stinking of cat pee. Jaz crossed the yard and headed for the canal bridge. The bridge was where the action was, everyone knew. On one side was the factory yard, on the other was the graveyard. That made it a lonely place. And the bridge made a dark brick tunnel. Ledges ran along either side of the black water. Jaz sat on one of the ledges now. A match flared against his face as he lit up. He sat and waited. He had Dennis's fifty quid in his pocket.

❖

'Hey, Jaz,' a voice said quietly. A figure sat down next to him.

'Spanner.'

Neither of them showed any surprise. Spanner did not need to ask if he wanted to buy. You only came down here if you did. 'How much you got?' the voice said.

'Fifty.'

Spanner nodded. 'This is the goods for fifty, OK?' He spread small plastic packets in the palm of his hand. Jaz chose quickly, handed over the full fifty, and stuffed the packets in his jeans pocket. The tall figure had already stood up. He backed out from under the bridge and vanished.

Jaz didn't see which way Spanner went up the bank, but guessed it would be the graveyard way.

He chose the factory yard instead. Just as well. There was a shout. An old bloke shouted his head off and tried to chase Spanner out of the graveyard.

Jaz looked back to see Spanner standing there with a stupid grin, while the old bloke got high blood pressure. 'What you up to? Go on, clear off. I'll get the police!'

Spanner gave him a little push backwards. The old bloke staggered up against a white stone cross. Then Spanner went off, dead slow, loping over the graves, giving the old bloke the V-sign.

Jaz winced, then shrugged. He ran through the factory yard and kicked a square metal chute. He listened to the echo and the squeal of a stray cat as it shot out of the end of the tube.

❖

Then Jaz let out a sigh and just stood there for a bit. This was the first time he'd done a deal with Spanner and he ought to be feeling good about it. Everyone knew Spanner, even the police. But they couldn't touch him, he was too clever. And they didn't care enough. Jaz knew he should have been pleased. With a pocket full of this stuff, he'd be king. He'd go up to the school gate and say to

Mark and Kiddy and Dom, 'Hey, let's go down to the graveyard.' They'd know what he meant. He'd be king, for at least a couple of days.

Jaz stood there in the factory yard, just thinking about things. Things like his mother's muffled voice from the front-room, and Dennis's lousy jacket stuffed with twenty-pound notes. He thought about his dad living in a pathetic bedsit on the other side of town, promising to take him to an Eric Clapton concert in the spring. Another cat, the colour of marmalade, but scrawny and lame, crept out of another tube. Jaz picked up half a brick and flung it at the cat. It hit metal. The echo set off rooks on the telephone wires, and they began cawing and flapping overhead.

❖

Jaz squeezed his eyes tight shut and roughly brushed his cheeks clear of tears. In a rage he tore Spanner's packets from his pocket, ripped them open and scattered them to the winds. He stamped them in the mud and leaves. He spat at them and fell back against a wall. When he finished sobbing, he thought his pockets were as empty as his heart. Like a robot he walked back into town, up the hill, to meet Mark and Kiddy and Dom.

2

Paying the Price

Talk about a let-down. 'Hey, Jaz,' they all said, 'you're for it now!'

'What do you mean?' He was lurking in Cross Street, waiting for the rest to come out of school.

'Hodgkins knows you bunked off,' Kiddy explained. Natalie Morris had her arm through Kiddy's. Jayne Somebody had linked up with Dom, and there was a girl called Mo from another class.

'Great. Anyhow, it's Friday. They'll have forgotten by Monday.' Jaz shrugged. 'Fancy a coffee?' He felt flat, empty, terrible. But he was still asking if they fancied a coffee. The girl called Mo smiled at him a bit as they walked down the hill. He didn't feel terrible enough not to see that she looked terrific and she was being nice to him.

'What did you do?' she asked. 'With your day off?'

'This and that.'

'Better than CDT?'

He nodded. He wasn't quite up to a grin.

'I like CDT,' she said.

'Yeah, you look artistic.' She wore loads of silver rings, and her hair wasn't a normal brown, more maroon.

'You coming in for a coffee?' he asked. This was putting himself out more than usual.

She shook her head. 'No, thanks. I've got something to do.'

He shrugged. It just wasn't his day. He went through the doorway of Highway Nine O, messing around with Mark, while Mo headed off. He noticed she looked nice from the back as well.

The estate was still parked outside when Jaz got back home. It was already dark, and cold as anything. His breath came out in a big cloud. He turned his key in the lock.

The swearing nearly knocked him straight back on to the street. Dennis was standing there with a stream of garbage coming out of his mouth. He pulled Jaz in, slammed the door shut and pinned him to it. The Yale lock stuck in Jaz's back.

'Where is it? Where is it?' Dennis snarled. Heather was leaning against the kitchen doorway, her hand covering her face.

'Where's what? What you on about?' Jaz knew lying wouldn't get him very far here, but you still had to try.

'The fifty quid, you little sod. Fifty quid, come on!' Dennis thumped Jaz's chest with every word. The Yale lock hurt his back.

'Give it to him, James, please!' Heather's face was red and puffy.

'What fifty quid?'

That was the last Jaz knew for a few minutes as Dennis let fly. He staggered under the big man's weight, went down on to his knees and covered his head. The worn carpet smelt old and damp. Dennis's shoes were the most polished ones he'd ever seen.

'Don't, Den, don't!' Heather's screams broke through the kicks. She tried to drag him off.

'Where is it?' Dennis said over and over. He pulled Jaz up to face level. His podgy white face had turned red with effort.

'I haven't got it!' Jaz dodged sideways. Dennis's fist met with the wall instead. Jaz stood up straight. 'I spent it,' he said calmly.

Dennis breathed out noisily, like the air coming out of a balloon. He nursed his fist in his left hand.

'See!' Heather shouted. 'He's admitted it. He spent it. Now leave him alone!'

Dennis aimed at her with his good hand. 'Stupid cow!' he said as he made contact with her face.

'I'll get the police on to him, just you wait!' He was out of the front door, into his car, on the car phone before she could even look into a mirror to see the damage to her face.

Jaz slammed the door. His mother was holding her face, sobbing like mad. She turned on him.

'Look what you've done! I'm going to tell your father. He'll have to deal with you now, just you wait!'

Wow, now I'm really frightened, Jaz thought. But he didn't say it. His dad couldn't deal with getting out of bed in the morning, let alone this crazy business.

❖

'He's done it this time, he's really done it!' his mum yelled, as if it were his dad's fault. 'He's ruined my life! You deal with him!'

'What's he done now?' His dad never raised his voice. He'd come over straight away.

'What's he done? Only skived school today, stolen fifty quid off Dennis and spent it on God knows what!' There was a big bruise coming up under her eye. 'Don't just stand there!' She was going crazy.

His dad *was* just standing there. Show him a feeling and he didn't know which way to turn. For his dad feelings were like headlights turned on a scared rabbit. He froze, waiting to be run over.

'What's happened?' he asked Jaz very slowly.

Jaz looked at him, greyer by the day, poorer, quieter, more frozen. 'Ask her, why don't you? Her boyfriend beat us up.' He nodded towards his mother. 'Said I nicked some cash.'

'Did you?'

Jaz gave a short sideways jerk of the head, meaning 'no'. Why should he make it easy?

❖

So Alan sat down on the front-room settee, took off his jacket and asked a few gentle questions. He never said, 'You little idiot, I'll tan your backside if I catch you doing this again!' He never looked as if he cared when Jaz told him what Dennis and his mum had been up to on that settee. He just said he'd scrape a bit more money together for them this month, and they could pay Dennis back with that.

Heather pulled herself together and nodded. Maybe she was already making plans for the fifty quid when she showed Alan to the door. A new dress, posh underwear.

Disgusted, Jaz made for the back door. He was out into the cold dark night before his dad's old Metro had coughed itself into life. He'd head for the canal, to see if anything was going on.

3

Rescue

His ribs ached from the kicking Dennis had given him. He saw himself in Patel's shop window, walking like an old man.

All the old men lay dead in the graveyard when he went in there. They turned their toes up to the stars in the cold and the dark. 'Ernest Simms. Born 4th June 1921. Died 21st March 1982. Beloved husband of Margaret.' And, 'In loving memory of Jason. Born 6th August 1962. Died 10th September 1962. Always in our hearts.' All the dead children too. Jaz kicked a white stone dove at the end of a grave. Then he did a little dance at death with a crushed Heineken can. He beat the defence, took a shot, wham! Right between the posts, goal!

His ribs felt stiff, though. He shoved his hands in his pockets and headed for the canal bridge.

There was this sudden high yell ripping through

the quiet night. A girl's voice, like she was being attacked, a splash, someone running, a car starting. Tyres screeched along the cement yard of the old factory. Headlights swung across the sooty brick walls, out through the gates. The girl's voice was still sounding in the dark, screaming, 'Bastards, bastards!' Jaz ran like mad over the bridge. He was glad the car had made its getaway. He didn't fancy another kicking.

❖

He saw a girl bent forward over the mucky canal water. He recognised her back view. It was Mo. She leant forward, but she couldn't reach what she wanted, down there in the stinking black water.

Jaz scrambled down the bank. 'You OK? What happened?' he said.

She stopped yelling. It didn't look like she was hurt. She ignored him, though.

'It's not safe down here at this time of the night!'

He sounded like his mother. He wanted to bite back what he'd just said. She'd think he was an idiot. Anyway, she was still lying there flat on her belly, reaching her pale arms out over the water.

'Don't just stand there!' Mo said. If he'd come to help, he'd better get a move on.

Now *she* sounded like his mother. 'What? Where?' He stared down in to the dark oily mess. The he heard it, a faint little crying noise, going on and on.

Mo's long hair was dripping wet from hanging in the water. She was scared. 'Get a stick, a piece of pipe, anything!' The crying grew fainter.

Jaz could see some kind of bag about a metre out into the water. It was slowly drifting further away.

'Kittens!' Mo said. 'They'll drown!'

No time for a stick then. Jaz just had time and sense to take off his leather jacket before he nipped over the edge into the water. It was waist deep. It flooded his trainers, sent foul air bubbles up his jeans. It was freezing.

He headed for the old sports bag. It was leaking water in and sinking like some old boat. The kittens must be at their last gasp. Jaz lunged for the bag – missed. Waves tipped it up further. Water flooded into it.

'Quick!' Mo yelled. She stood and pointed. Jaz scooped up three little drowned rat things, two in one hand, one in the other. They felt slimy. 'There!' She pointed to a fourth. Its head was just above the surface. Jaz grabbed it. It cried weakly. He waded back to the bank with four wailing babies.

❖

His ribs hurt again as he handed Mo the kittens. She rolled them up inside his nice dry jacket. 'Hey!' he shouted. She just clicked her tongue and took no notice. 'They OK?' he asked.

She tutted again. 'No thanks to you.'

'What are you on about?' He'd just done his Superman act, rescued the weak and helpless. He was a hero. He climbed up on to the bank, shivering.

'A long stick would have done the trick, like I said. I could've hitched it through the handles and lifted the whole thing out. But no, you have to jump in and tip them all out. You half-drowned them!'

'I just saved their lives!' He was freezing. His jeans felt like wet cardboard.

'Hm.' Mo didn't seem to care. Gently she rubbed the kittens with the soft material of her skirt. She fluffed them up, snuggled them inside the warm lining of his jacket.

Jaz went to look and bent over them. He decided they'd been worth saving after all. 'How old are they, then?'

'About eight weeks. Two tabbies, one black, one tortoiseshell, see!'

'Come again?'

'Never mind.' She looked over at him for the first time and smiled. 'Thanks,' she said.

Her smile was like an electric fire shooting warmth all through his body.

'How come you know so much about them?' Her long fingers gently pressed the kittens' paws and legs to see if anything was broken. 'Who dumped them in there, anyway?'

She shrugged. 'Never seen them before. Someone in a Volvo.' She laughed. 'H reg.' Mo could see he didn't get it. 'They want to get rid of them. Can't be bothered to find a proper home for them. They drive down here, drop them in the canal while no one's looking. Finish. Loads of people do it.'

'That so?' he grunted. People needed their heads looking at. The kittens weren't crying now. They were sleeping, snuggled in the sleeve hole of his jacket. 'What about you?' he asked Mo. 'What were you doing down here?'

'Ah!' she said. She picked up the sleeping bundle, stood straight, and nodded across the yard to the empty factory. 'Come with me!'

4

Mo's Secret

Mo led Jaz inside through a low window with no glass in it. It was pitch dark. The place smelt of petrol and filth.

'Here,' Mo whispered. He took the warm armful of kittens. She found a torch in her pocket and lit their way.

'Watch out!' She pointed to low metal girders, holes in the concrete floor. She swung the torch beam on to all the danger spots.

'You've been here before.'

She said nothing, just crossed the old factory floor. They ignored the broken glass, the piles of rotting rags. Mo made for the far corner. 'Give them to me now,' she said.

They stopped and the torch went off. He handed her the kittens. He had to get used to the dark again. Above his head he felt a grey shape glide along a girder. Beneath his feet, something else slid past. His eyes began to see in the dark. He saw other eyes. Yellow ones, glinting. Three, four, five pairs. Cats' eyes.

'See!' Mo said.

He watched her bend down and put the kittens one by one into a cardboard box lined with newspaper. Mo gave him his jacket, still warm from the kittens' bodies. He was glad to put it back on. In one corner of the box there was a saucer full of milk. Other saucers lined the wall. More cats came and drank as Mo undid a carton and poured more milk. It was all set out, cans of food, piles of fresh newspaper, a can opener. Jaz looked into the box and saw his kittens happily drinking.

'You fixed all this?' he asked her.

She nodded. 'I come down here very day. Twice a day when there's kittens.'

'Who do they belong to?'

'Nobody.'

'They wild?'

'No. Just homeless. People buy them or are given them, but then they get fed up. Sometimes they can't afford to feed them. Whatever.' She was busy now with fresh saucers of food.

'So how can you – afford it?' Jaz had noticed the neat rows of canned food. Maybe she'd nicked them and her halo would slip. No one could be this perfect.

Then again, maybe they could. She looked up and saw he was still shivering. She came and sat on the metal ledge next to him.

'I work two evenings a week at Highway, as a waitress. It pays for the food.' She stopped to think. 'I want to raise more money for a proper shelter, though.'

This was weird. He was sitting shivering next to a girl who got prettier every time he looked at her. She had pale eyes and they looked wide in this dark, empty place. She had pale skin, and long, dark hair. Silver shone at her ears and throat, and on her long fingers. She was nutty about cats. She was talking to him. He couldn't believe this.

'What about you?' she asked. 'What are you doing down here at this time of night?'

❖

At first he just shrugged. You couldn't say, 'I hate my mother. My father's a dead loss.' It made you sound like a little kid.

'Had a row at home?' She knew all about that. The family wages going straight down the betting shop, her mother screaming she needed sixty quid for the electricity bill or they'd be cut off.

Jaz nodded.

'That why you nicked off school today?'

'No. The row came after.' He told her about the fifty quid. That would put her off him, he expected. He stood up to go.

Then, 'Don't go,' Mo said gently. She took his hand. He sat down again in the dark. Cats purred against their legs.

For a second he saw himself as just another stray cat. Another animal she wanted to rescue. He felt mad with her. Who did she think she was, going around adopting strays? Then he looked at her face again and listened to her. She'd been there, done all that, she said. All the family scenes and let-downs, and running away just so you didn't have to look at their stupid faces putting on their stupid make-up or shaving their stupid chins. He looked and saw her wide open eyes, the glint of silver earring, and he had to kiss her.

❖

She told him a story from her life. She sat close, leaning against his sore ribs. He never told her it hurt.

'It's not a long story,' Mo promised. 'Sure you

want to hear it?'

'Is it about cats?'

'No, idiot!' She pushed sideways against his ribs.

'Ouch!' He couldn't help it.

'What?'

'Nothing.'

'Right, then. My dad once had a win on the horses. Most of the time he lost, right? But one day he came home with a stupid grin from ear to ear, totally smashed out of his head, mind you. "Let's all go on holiday!" he says. My mum doesn't believe him. She's heard it all before. It's six years since we had a holiday, before my little brother was born even. "Honest!" my dad says. "We can afford it!" He waves this massive bunch of notes in our faces. "Abroad. Spain! Costa Brava. Costa Packet!" He gives her the money for the deposit. She buys my little brother some beach shoes. We borrow suitcases from my aunty.'

Mo stooped to stroke a grey cat from ear to tail. 'We're all packed to go. My dad is on his way home. We're setting off at 11 that night from Manchester. But he pops in to William Hill's on the way as usual. He never pops out again. Blew the whole lot – air fares, hotel money, the lot! Couldn't face coming home to my mum. William Hill's shut the door on him at 5. We never saw him again.'

'No?'

Mo nodded. 'Never. Good riddance, my mum said in the end. She took us all to the seaside the next day. Said my little brother would get to wear his beach shoes if it killed her. She says she's better off knowing where she stands now. She wouldn't have my dad back if he walked in the door with a million pounds.'

❖

Jaz listened in silence. You couldn't help kissing someone who looked and sounded like she did. Not sorry for herself. He told her about Dennis, said he wished his mum was more like hers.

Mo put her hand on his side when he told her how Dennis had kicked his ribs. 'They'll be bruised,' she said.

'They'll mend.'

'You can't choose your parents.' She sounded really sad when she said that. He still felt her hand on his side, even when they'd walked back out of the factory, down by the canal, over the bridge, and up into town.

❖

Amazing how you acted normal again when you met up with Dom and Jayne and Kiddy. Even when you were holding hands with a brilliant girl, and you'd just had the best conversation you'd ever had in your whole life, and you wanted to kiss her again, and you felt you could never keep your hands off her, but you had to. He must've been grinning all over his face when Kiddy said, 'Hi, you two. Fancy a game of pool?' and Jayne said something about the cat that got the cream.

'Yeah, sure,' Jaz said. 'Me and Mo will thrash you at pool, won't we?'

They went off together, as if it were a normal night. No life-saving, no miracles, nothing.

5

The Police

He should have checked the front of his house before he went back in. It would have made sense. But he'd had a great night, he was feeling fine, and so he slipped in the back way. He didn't want to meet up with Heather, his dear mother, with her black eye and his dad's fifty quid burning a hole in her pocket.

'James!' She heard the door shut.

Her voice sounded weird. He went into the front room. There were two big men in big blue uniforms with big boots and big voices.

'James Taylor?' one of them asked.

He wanted to say 'No', swear his head off, run away. But he stood fixed to the puke green carpet, not saying a word.

'James!' His mum came forward. She looked a mess.

One of the policemen moved forward even faster and pushed her to one side.

'It is James, then?'

He said nothing. He raised his chin, looked sideways at the man. 'So what if it is?' he said with his body, hands in pockets, looking down his nose. He could see their car outside the front door. If only he'd checked.

'We want to talk to you about the theft of some money earlier today.' The policeman sounded as if it happened every day.

Heather stood there looking like it was an earthquake. 'It's all a big mistake,' she gabbled. 'James can explain, can't you, James?' She dredged some words out of the back of her head. 'It was a family row!'

The second policeman stared at her, took her back to the settee and sat her down. He shook his head.

The first one kept on at Jaz. 'We've had a complaint from a Mr Dennis Waring. He says you stole fifty pounds from his wallet. He came in and signed a statement. Wants us to press charges.' He looked steadily at Jaz's chin.

Jaz was saying nothing.

'Ever been in trouble before?'

Still nothing.

'How old are you?'

'Fourteen!' his mother sobbed. 'He's only fourteen!'

'Old enough to know better.' There was a big pause. Jaz's nerve was going. It was the long stare that was getting to him. At school they just put you in detention and forgot about you. You could skive, 'borrow' someone's pen, cheek a teacher, whatever. They just barked 'Detention!' at you. That was it, and you went away.

'Did you take it, this fifty quid?' the policeman asked.

'He doesn't have to answer! Don't answer that, James!' His mum leapt up, still crying all over the place.

'Mrs Taylor!' The other one was losing his temper. He took her out of the room.

'You've upset your mum now.'

Jaz stared up at the ceiling.

'Don't care, do you?'

Jaz looked down at the pukey carpet.

'Where's your dad?'

'Not here.' The answer leapt out of his throat.

The policeman weighed it up. 'And this Mr Waring, where's he fit in?'

'Ask her!' Jaz clenched his teeth.

'Boyfriend?' The policeman asked, casual and insulting.

'So?'

'He doesn't like you much, your mum's boyfriend. Have you been giving him hassle?'

❖

Jaz was losing the staring battle. 'I never take no notice.' he said, weakening.

'Stay out of the way, do you?'

He nodded.

'But not today? He says you took fifty from his wallet.'

'He says.'

'Did you?'

'Prove it!'

The policeman's eyes went cool. He dropped the friendly mood. 'Maybe we will.' He dropped the stare. His voice was more like a robot's. 'We could take you down now and charge you.'

Jaz's chin was up again.

'Anyhow, we know where you live. We know who you are. You won't be going far, will you?' He headed for the kitchen to collect his mate. They were out of the house, in their car, taking the next radio call, moving off, before Jaz drew another breath. His mother came back in with a streamer of kitchen roll for her leaking eyes.

'Where did I go wrong?' She said over and over, like some chant. 'I did something wrong for you to turn out like this!'

'Everything,' Jaz said.

It sent her crazy. 'I gave you everything! You never went without! I was the one who went without, not you. Not your lousy father. Me! Why should I? I've got a life of my own, haven't I? What's wrong with that? I can have men friends, can't I? I'm allowed. Ask your father about his girlfriends, why don't you! Are you listening to me, James? I said I've got a life of my own, haven't I?'

Her face was red and puffed up with tears.

'And now the police! I've never had the police round in all my life! That's enough! That's it, you've gone too far, you can just get out of here, go on, get out!' She was screaming at him.

'Right,' Jaz said, very quiet.

She stopped screaming. 'What?' She screwed the kitchen roll into a ball.

'I said, right.' Jaz felt calm. He headed for the back door.

Heather caught his sleeve, dragged him back. 'Don't be silly. I didn't mean it, I'm upset. James!'

He never stopped or looked back.

❖

It was 12 o'clock, midnight. Next door would hear the door slam. Heather ran for the phone.

'Dennis, it's me! I don't know what to do. It's James, he's walked out. I don't know. He's run away. Den, what am I going to do?'

From the safety of a town seventy miles down the motorway, Dennis gave her comfort and advice. He called her 'love', said he'd see her at 2 o'clock next Tuesday afternoon.

❖

Friday turned into Saturday. Dreams turned into despair. Jaz had walked into that house dreaming of Mo – her voice, her laugh, her way of saying, 'Been there, done that. No problem.'

He walked out feeling like death. Mo and her cats, and the kittens he'd rescued, they all belonged to a different world drifting out of reach; like that old sports bag in the canal. You couldn't be a hero and rescue your own life from drifting, drowning. Jaz walked into the dead town centre. No cars, no lights in the shops. He slid down an alley while a car cruised past, waited in the shadow. When he came out on to the street again, all he saw was the lean, lonely figure of Spanner.

'Hey,' Spanner nodded. Black T-shirt, black jeans. The orange street light flickered. Spanner smelt business. He nodded Jaz in the direction of the graveyard. 'Meet you in five minutes,' he said. 'First I gotta see a man.'

6

At the Station

❖

He didn't care about Spanner, but the canal side drew him down. Jaz sat on the low graveyard wall, propped against the iron railings. He was backed up against the ghostly white angels and crosses. The black water oozed at his feet. He had a weird idea that Mo was floating by in a boat, her pale face smiling. But he couldn't reach her, she was only a dream. She turned her face towards him and waved, with all her silver rings. Rings on her fingers.

He remembered the nursery rhyme. 'Rings on her fingers and bells on her toes, She shall have music...' His mum had told him that when he was little. Mo's dreaming face vanished in the black tunnel of the arch. Only a grey cat padded in real life along the wall, ignoring Jaz.

'Hey,' Spanner said again. He sat, silent as any

cat. 'How much you wanna spend this time?'

'Got no money,' Jaz said without looking up.

Spanner flicked his thumb across one eyebrow, like he was swatting a fly. 'You're joking,' he said.

'No.'

'What did you want a meet for, then? You enjoy wasting my time?'

Jaz shrugged. 'Thought it was your idea.'

'Yeh, but I'm not Santa Claus with a sack full of goodies. What did you expect, presents?' Spanner toed the earth. He thought for a few seconds 'Mind you, I like you. You're a good kid.'

How would you know? Jaz thought. He remembered Spanner at school a couple of years back. Always the big guy, with his hair slicked back, the one you never crossed. He already had a name for dealing drugs, even then. The school knew, everyone knew. They didn't chuck him out, though. Maybe they were scared. He left the place in his own good time, went off for a year, came back to town in the black gear, with black dyed hair. The really big guy now. Every day he stood at the school gate waiting for customers.

Spanner took one of his small plastic packets out of his back pocket. He began to open it with his long fingers. His thin face bent forwards. 'Try this,' he offered – like, 'have a fag, have a beer,' completely normal, between mates.

❖

You could say 'Yes', like falling off a log. You'd be in with the crowd then, mostly older kids. Kiddy and Mark would whistle through their teeth when he told them. 'You never!' they'd say. And he'd be able to tell them. 'It was like floating,' he'd say. 'Like you were looking down, and everything was too far away to touch, and bright colours. The whole world looked great!' He'd heard it all before.

'Go on,' Spanner said. 'Suck it and see.' The kid would bring him new customers, he'd tell his mates. They'd save their paper-round money until they had enough to buy whatever he was selling. He grinned at Jaz. 'Go on, try it!' Jaz's fingers itched to take it.

Then the siren started. The blue light flashed in the factory yard. Two figures were running over the bridge.

Spanner swore and sprang up. He fumbled, and began to empty his pockets into the water, but not quickly enough. The police were there, shoving his arm up his back until he yelped. They slapped their big hands over him, found the packets stashed away, money everywhere. Fifty quid floated in the water.

The only free bit of Spanner's body was his legs. He leaned back and, like a cat that's trapped, he arched and kicked out at Jaz. 'Stupid kid!' he screamed. He landed both feet on Jaz's chest. Jaz staggered, caught his heel on the wall, fell sideways. For the second time that night he hit the scummy water, felt its icy smack. This time, the old bill hauled him out.

❖

They didn't have to tell him this was big trouble. They didn't need to drag him dripping wet down the station to tell him possession of drugs was a serious offence. 'Search me, why don't you!' he yelled. 'I know how it must look!' He spread the palms of his hands upwards. 'So search me!'

'We know, you're innocent. Yeh, yeh.' They nodded their heads.

Jaz felt sick as the man body-searched him.

'Dry him off, hang on to him.' Then they left the yellow office. It had posters on the walls telling you to lock your car. Someone chucked a dry shirt and trousers in. He got changed. They hung off him like clown clothes. 'Jesus,' he thought. 'What next?'

'Right!' The body searcher came back at about 3 in the morning. Jaz could see now he was the one who'd come to the house about Dennis's fifty quid. 'This is some night you're having, James.' He shoved Jaz's wet jeans, shirt and jacket into a bin bag. 'Come on, then!' He held the door open.

'Where we going?' Jaz felt like a whale had swallowed him back there in the canal. Some monster whose belly you swam around in and couldn't get out of. 'I never took any of it off him! Spanner wanted to give me some stuff. I never even knew what it was!' Jaz knew he sounded desperate. 'I never said yes!'

'Prove it,' the policeman said. 'You thought that was *your* line, didn't you?'

The truth tumbled out of Jaz's mouth, all broken and twisted.

'Listen, maybe I did borrow the fifty quid from Dennis. I never saw it as stealing. I never thought he'd come to you about it. He gives my mum money all the time.'

Again he felt sick. He watched the smile on the old bill's face. He knew what that kind of smile meant.

'It's OK.' The man decided it was time to stop giving Jaz a hard time. 'Mr Waring rang us up around midnight, said he wasn't going to press charges.'

It sank in. No charges! Jaz nearly cried. The policeman pushed the bag of wet clothes at him and showed him the front door, really polite.

'We rang your mum to tell her the good news. She said you'd run off. We told her we'd keep an eye open. That was you down by the canal, wasn't it?'

Jaz nodded.

'Like we said, we kept an eye open.' He paused again and gave one of his stares. 'That's bad company you're keeping, you know that?'

'Are you going to charge me for it, then?' The fresh air had hit Jaz in the face. 'Or what?'

'We haven't decided. We're still talking to your friend here. We'll let you know.'

They didn't need to tell him a second time. The whale had belched him out in one of those great jets of water that come out of their heads. He took a deep breath.

'Go straight home,' the big man said. He was the sort of father you'd have if you did all you homework on time and visited your gran on a Sunday. He'd been a boy scout or a policeman all his life.

Jaz walked down the street without looking back. He didn't go straight home, though. 'Home' was the last place he wanted to go.

7

Nothing to Lose

❖

Jaz walked quickly across town, taking the short cuts. He'd never been out in the dead of night before, in the damp streets. His clown trousers flapped round his ankles.

His dad's flat was in a basement, down six concrete steps. The curtains only came halfway down the french doors. Jaz bent down low enough to see his dad stretched out on the bed-settee. The TV screen flickered and whined. He rapped on the window. His dad groaned, turned, sat up.

'Dad, it's me!'

'Jaz?' He opened the door, bleary-eyed. What time is it? What's wrong?'

'Nothing. Here, grab this.' Jaz handed him the bag of wet clothes.

'Man, what you got on!' Alan pointed at his trousers.

'Ha, ha, very funny!'

His dad still lived in the seventies. He said, 'Man' and 'Wow' and 'Hey!'

'Where's that fan heater thing?' Jaz got busy drying his stuff. 'What happens to leather when you dry it out?'

'It cracks.'

'It stinks!' Jaz flung his jacket down, disgusted. His dad found a hanger for it, and went to hang it in the shower cubicle. Jaz told him the whole story as he got back into his own jeans and let them steam dry on him. He missed out the bit about Mo and the cats, though.

'You say Dennis rang the police?' Alan sat on the edge of the table, drinking coffee. It took ages for things to sink in. 'He withdrew the charges?'

Why did he look so grey and slow? His brain cells were leaking out by the million.

'Then you shouted at Heather?'

'She shouted at me.'

'You ran off and the police picked you up again. For some drugs deal? Who's this Spanner guy?'

❖

What did it matter? He just wanted his dad to jump

straight up, say he'd sort them all out, give Dennis and Spanner a good belting. Fat chance. Even when he was a little kid, his dad would listen, nod, talk and listen. He never did anything. He was a plastic man. You had to move his arms and legs and put him into the right position, just to sit him up. Jaz felt hopeless.

'Does Heather know where you are?' Alan asked. 'Shall I ring up and tell her? Or let's leave it till morning, OK? She'll be asleep. What d'you think, Jaz; now or later?'

'Later,' Jaz said. He watched his father settle down to finish off his night's sleep. He sat there in the slow dawn. What did you do when nowhere was the right place to go?

❖

They made phone calls. They talked. His parents decided Jaz should stay put for the weekend at his dad's place.

'You've got to help me sort him out,' Heather told Alan. 'He's your son!' She slammed the phone down.

But she couldn't leave it at that. She kept on ringing back. 'Listen, what are you going to do about him? I can't have him stealing things from the house, can I? Why don't you go in to the school on Monday to sort things out? Why not? Listen, I'm asking you, what are you going to do about your son?' Slam went the phone.

'By the way,' she said. It was the fifth phone call of the day. 'Tell him some girl called Mo rang here asking for him. She left a number.'

Jaz felt the name batter at his numb heart. But he took the number from his dad and shoved it down the bog. He was trying not to think of Mo. She was like a promise that couldn't be kept. Better to say 'No' in the first place.

At 6 o'clock the phone rang again. Alan answered it. 'Jaz, there's this girl, Mo, on the phone. Heather gave her the number. She wants to talk to you.'

Jaz was in the shower, getting the smell of the canal out of his hair. Alan passed on a message. 'He can't speak right now, he's busy. Sorry.'

Jaz heard him put the phone down, and felt the sad, empty click it made on his mind

❖

It was down by the canal he felt clearest, even if it was raining. He could see Dom hanging round by the bridge, felt like going up to him and saying,

'Steer clear. Don't get mixed up with Spanner and his lot.' But Spanner was down at the police station, remember? And who was he, Jaz, to be handing out the advice?

Dom looked 14, going on 40, with his little thin face and his nose that was too big for it. He had mousy brown-grey hair. No one showed up, and Dom wandered off in the drizzle. Jaz went under the bridge arch and squatted on the ledge, where it was dry.

If someone had come up and said, 'Hey, you're not thinking of jumping in and ending it all, are you?' he'd have sworn and told them to get lost, said what a stupid idea. In his head he thought about death by drowning, like it was an idea he was having for someone else. How long would it take? Would it hurt?

❖

Someone came and sat down beside him. It was Mo. 'Don't do it,' she said, with a grin. She pushed him and pretended to save him, then sat there hugging him without saying anything.

She never broke in when he told her about his dad being a wimp and his mum being a slag. He told her about Spanner and the drug deals.

'If I'd just had another second to think about it, I'd have said yeh, OK, and taken the tabs. The police would've got me for doing drugs, and I'd be in it up to my ears for sure.'

'Maybe.'

'Yeh, I would.'

'Who says?'

'I know me. I've got nothing to lose.'

Mo looked down at her own hands, said nothing.

Jaz kicked himself. 'I mean, I *had* nothing to lose. Before. I didn't mean you, honest!' She looked quiet and far away, like she'd put up walls.

'You never rang me,' she reminded him.

'I never thought you wanted to hear. I didn't want to tell you anyway. Drugs. Spanner. My lousy mum and dad.'

❖

'Come on,' Mo said, 'feeding time!' She could just break his mood by getting up and going.

They walked together under the arch and up into the old factory. Jaz had the mad idea of scrambling up a pile of old metal chutes, up on to the roof. He balanced like a tightrope walker. 'Look!'

He wanted to show off. If she said 'Fly!' he'd fly. She watched his black shape against the grey sky, then turned and climbed in through the broken window. He came down, wet and winded. 'Well?'

'Open that tin,' Mo said. The cats were weaving in and out of boxes and beams, rubbing up against her. His kittens miaowed for food.

Jaz sighed.

'What's wrong?' She smacked the saucers down on the concrete with smart little movements, mashing the food with a fork.

'Nothing. I thought you'd go for the dicing with death bit.'

'Up on the roof?'

'Yeh.'

He looked so miserable, picking up his black kitten and poking it, that she smiled and said, 'I did!' and gave him a corny look.

He laughed at himself.

'No, stroke him like this.' She showed him the proper way.

'Don't you think he's a bit skinny?' Jaz could feel its ribs.

'He's fine. He's eating, no problem, look.' They made sure each kitten got its share. 'You fancy helping me to raise money for this proper shelter, then?' Mo asked.

He nodded. 'Don't mention it to that Natalie, though. She'll go round gabbing to everyone.' What was he saying? He was making plans, thinking about tomorrow.

'Don't rush me,' he said. One step forward, half a step back.

'It's getting dark.' Mo stood by a window. She looked cold. He went over and put his arm round her. 'I think it's all a bit like learning to see in the dark. You know, like cats' eyes.'

'What is?'

'Making plans. Looking ahead. Like the future is a really dark place and you can't see ahead. But you learn, like cats learn, and you get your balance, and soon your eyes get used to the dark.'

'Meaning?' He just wanted to go on holding her. She smelt of flowers, and she gleamed silver here in this filthy place.

'Meaning, I want us to make plans. Let's get some money together for the shelter. Say yes!'

She shall have music. 'Yes' sounded like notes in a song. Her laugh was a guitar solo. She rode through life with her silver rings, smiling. Wherever she goes. 'But don't rush me,' he said. 'You don't change the habits of a life-time overnight.'

8

More Trouble from Spanner

Mo even brought a smile to Alan's face. A slow smile. She did that all the time: made sad people happy. She told him the basement flat was her idea of heaven. You didn't have to get out of bed to brush your teeth or cook a can of beans.

'No room to swing a cat,' Alan agreed.

Mo and Jaz raised their eyebrows and laughed.

'Hey, what did I say?'

'Nothing.'

Smiling was catching. They all sat round grinning like idiots. Alan said even the yard outside was bigger than the flat.

'He kept *you* quiet,' Alan told Mo when Jaz went

out to the shop for a carton of milk. 'He had me pretty worried for a bit back there. I mean, I don't mind the odd joint, but there's hard drugs round this town. And he's been hanging out down by the canal. And then the police and all that stuff. His mother's been going crazy.'

'I know.' Mo wondered why parents always worried about the wrong things. She didn't ask.

When Mo came back, she and Jaz arranged to meet up at the old factory next day.

'After tea. I've got to babysit my kid brother till then,' she said.

All Sunday with nothing to do. Jaz looked down in the mouth.

'I'm gonna paint this wall in here,' his dad said. 'Dulux brilliant white. Wanna help?'

'Great.'

'Don't get too excited, man. Then on Monday I'll go in and sort out this school thing, see this Mr Hodgkiss your mum was on about.'

'Don't bother,' Jaz said. 'I can do it.'

Mo looked at Alan and nodded. 'No problem.'

Alan said 'OK' and left the two of them to say goodbye on the basement steps.

'He's OK, your dad,' she told Jaz. 'He knows when not to poke his nose in.'

Funny, though, Jaz couldn't kiss Mo goodbye,

not here on his dad's steps. 'See you tomorrow,' he said, dead shy.

❖

He was there early to feed the cats. Animals learnt things really quickly, like who would feed them and look after them. They trusted you.

And they heard trouble before you did. Jaz was just putting a kitten back in its box when the other cats melted away like magic. They slunk off without finishing their food. The grey one crept up on a beam and hissed.

Jaz looked down the length of the factory floor. Rays of grey light slanted in through the bare windows. He saw a black figure against a window frame. He'd recognise Spanner anywhere. The spidery outline moved towards him. Other shapes filled the window frame - three, four of Spanner's gang. The grey cat spat. The kittens miaowed in their box.

'Hey,' Spanner greeted Jaz, very sinister. The gang moved in behind.

Jaz looked round. He was cornered. He jumped for the beam up alongside the grey cat, pulled himself up and sat astride the metal support. He looked down at Spanner.

Spanner looked up. 'They let me out,' he explained. 'This morning.'

'Great,' Jaz said, through gritted teeth.

'On bail.' He was wearing an empty grin.

Another pause.

'Just until they bring the case to court.'

Silence. Jaz perched on his beam. The four kids behind Spanner had fanned out. He would have to balance along the beams and head for a patch of daylight, up on to the broken roof, to make his getaway.

'Possession. Dealing. The works.' His voice sounded too flat, too calm. 'I could get two years. You set me up for it,' he told Jaz. 'The old bill followed you and they nicked me. They let you go. Thanks a lot.'

No use hanging round to say it wasn't his fault, he hadn't planned it that way. Who'd believe him? He saw Spanner give a signal. The gang began to scramble up boxes, on to beams, like monkeys. Jaz grabbed for a ledge running high along the side wall, swung on to it and made for the daylight in the roof. All kinds of rubbish and loose metal crashed to the floor, but he was faster than them, he was getting away.

❖

'Wait!' Spanner's voice cut the air. The gang froze. 'Leave him. Come back here.' They did as they were told. 'Just take a look here!' His voice sneered. He was staring into the box with the kittens.

'Ah, cute!' The crying of the kittens swamped Spanner's voice as he grabbed each one in turn and tossed it like a rugby ball at a member of his gang.

'Don't do that!' Jaz yelled down at them. They ignored him, headed for the open air. They ran with the kittens. Jaz came up on to the roof, stood wide-legged on the slates to watch the gang head for the water.

'Come back here!' He slid twenty feet down the slope, taking slates with him. He swung on to a drainpipe, shinned down. They were at the water's edge. They were going to chuck the kittens in!

Jaz pelted across the yard. 'Stop that!' They held the kittens out above the water. Spanner stood and faced him, with a grin from ear to ear.

'Or else?'

'Put them back!' He was mad. They'd got his cats. They'd better not dump them back in that canal. He charged right at Spanner, made contact with his belly. He tackled him down to the ground. The others stood round, caught by surprise. The kid was mad, he was thumping Spanner, using his legs too. He was bleeding from the mouth. The kid was crazy.

Spanner fought back. 'Dump them!' he kept gasping. 'Go on, dump them!'

Jaz gasped for the breath that Spanner was kicking out of him. As long as he went on fighting, the gang would stand there staring. They wouldn't dump the kittens. He had to fight on. He got up. Head down, he butted Spanner in the guts again. Spanner brought his knee up and smacked Jaz on the chin.

'Dump them! Dump them!' Spanner screamed. The kittens howled.

❖

Other feet came running across the bridge, along the canal side. Everyone was yelling, fighting, splashing - then Spanner's gang was running. Kittens were in the water, but Dom and Kiddy and Mark were scooping them out again. The gang had dumped Spanner now. They took off along the path, through the weeds and nettles, back towards town.

Through the slits that were once his eyes, Jaz

saw them run. He saw his mates pick up the four kittens, and only then did he let go of Spanner. He felt one last kick in the ribs, heard Spanner run. That was all he knew before Dom came, held his bleeding face out of the dirt, and told Kiddy to call an ambulance, quick.

9

Something Better

When he came round someone else was holding his hand. Mo. Tears streamed down her face. The white hospital lights hurt his eyes. He tried to shift his head sideways.

'He'll be all right now,' a woman's voice said. 'Doctor will be along shortly. Just keep him nice and quiet.'

Mo held his head and stroked his face. She wasn't saying anything.

The doctor came, Jaz was just another kid who'd got himself beaten up. He patched Jaz up, and sent him for an X-ray.

'Where are the parents?' he said in a voice that sounded like every teacher, every policeman everywhere.

'No,' Jaz said. He didn't want his mum and dad.

'Ssh, they're on their way,' Mo said.

The doctor grunted and left.

'I saw what you did,' Mo whispered. And that made everything all right again. 'I'm sorry I was late.'

'I was early.'

'Anyway, here's Alan and your mum.'

'Don't go,' Jaz said, just seeing the gleam of silver on her fingers, feeling the rings cool against his face. Mo bent down and kissed him as Alan and Heather came up to the bed.

'Oh God!' Heather stuffed a fist into her mouth. His face was terrible; all swollen and cut and stitched.

'Ssh,' Alan said. He talked quietly to Mo about how it had all happened.

'Been a hero, our kid?' he said to Jaz. 'We just saw the doctor. No bones broken. They'll check things out for concussion, keep you in overnight, then we can take you home.'

Home. The word fell like a stone to the bottom of the black canal.

'To your dad's place,' Heather cut in. She'd got over the shock. 'We've talked it over. Your dad can look after you better, the way things are.'

He was glad, but it hurt like hell. He tried to look his mother full in the face, but she couldn't meet his gaze. Dennis was more important to her, and the big car, and the money, and the long-distance phone calls.

'You can come and visit whenever you like. It's just across town after all, not far. And maybe it won't be for long.' She trailed off.

'Well,' she said to the others, 'I've been looking after him for fourteen years. Now let someone else have a go!' She left before anyone could argue. She went off down the ward in her high heels, click-click-clack.

'Who cares?' Jaz told himself. 'I left that stinking place. She never threw me out. I left!' It was the best he could do.

'Get some rest,' Alan said. 'I'll be back for you in the morning, soon as they open those doors.' He left Mo to say goodbye in private.

'I'm glad,' she told him.

He could see her dark hair framing her face, falling over one shoulder. 'What?'

'You saved the cats.'

'Course.' He reminded her about Dom and the others. They were great, she agreed.

'And I'm glad you're going to live in the flat. It's nearer my place.'

'Hey!' Jaz said. He felt strong enough to prop himself upon the pillow.

'And!' Mo said. Her face lit up with a new secret.

'What? Go on, tell me!'

'You know there's that big yard at the back of your dad's place...?'

❖

Jaz had the worst night he'd ever known. Old men cried out in the dark, and nutters wandered around without their pyjamas.

So it really made his day when the policeman he knew all too well headed for his bedside. Jaz was in the middle of soggy cornflakes and burnt toast.

'James Taylor?' He had to check the record card to make sure. 'You're a sight for sore eyes.' Jaz's face had changed since Saturday. 'Just come to say there's no charge against you. No possession, no causing a fight. It wasn't your fault. We've got witnesses, OK?' He spoke loud, as if it were Jaz' s ears that were broken. Or his brain.

'Thanks,' Jaz said.

'Just thought you'd like to know.' The policeman moved off. 'Oh, and your mate, Spanner, is it?'

Jaz nodded.

'He's nicked again. On remand this time. Tucked up nice and cosy down the station.'

Jaz nodded again. He managed to crack a smile through the cuts and bruises. 'Thanks.'

Later Alan came in with a set of clean clothes. Jaz left that place as quickly as his stiff legs would carry him. His dad's old Metro just made it from the hospital to the flat. As they went down the steps, it already felt like home.

'Flowers?' Jaz said. There was a jug of roses on the table by the TV.

'From Mo.' He looked at his son. 'She'll be round straight after school.'

Jaz cracked another painful grin.

'Hey, and I've been thinking,' Alan said. 'You know this big old yard we've got out the back here? Well, why don't you help that girl of yours fix up a proper cats' home out there? A proper lean-to, with dry places for them to sleep. Nothing fancy. A little box for the kittens you pick up down by the canal. Better than the draughty old factory!'

'Wow, and you thought that up all by yourself?' Jaz asked, still grinning.

'Yeh. Well, I talked to Mo, of course. She thinks it's a great idea!'

'Bet she does. Well, it is,' Jaz agreed, wrapping his hand around a hot cup of coffee.

❖

He already knew her footsteps when Mo came down at just gone 4. She said he still looked like Frankenstein. He ignored that.

'I'll make that shelter while I'm off school,' he said.

'Great. I'll bring your kittens up soon as it's ready.'

'Tomorrow.'

'No, I want a proper place, properly done,' she said.

❖

They measured things and added things up. 'We'll make a sign,' he said. 'Mo's Place for Stray Cats.'

'What for?' She hitched her hair behind one ear and stared at him. 'I can do a logo. A cat with a roof over its head. In CDT. Hodgkins will be really impressed!'

'Fine,' Mo said, laughing her head off. 'Mo's Place for Stray Cats.'